George Ambrose, 33
English Teacher

My heart must rise and go now, to that
    bright Harlem street
Where buildings trued in ragtime and
    Congo rhythms meet
I'll build a storefront church there, spread
    amens through the pews
Snatch up my cross and gladly tithe my dues

Here will I find the sainted, the weak ones
    and the strong
A thousand mournful voicings, one sweet
    and tender song
Midnight gives its saucy call, a full moon
    offers light
Finger-snapping angels rock the night

My heart must rise and go now,
    for now the choirs come
And now the skies are parting and now
    the guitars strum
I take my stand in Harlem, and sing of jubilee
Here my fretful soul flies wondrous free

Here in Harlem
poems in many voices

APARTMENTS TO LET.

3 or 4 Rooms with Improvements
For Respectable Colored Families Only.
Inquire of
Janitor or J. PALETZ, 314 7th AVE.
Telephone 1858-CHELSEA

Here in Harlem

poems in many voices

written by

Walter Dean Myers

Holiday House / *New York*

To Constance

The front jacket photograph is of Duke Ellington and two of his singers c. 1938.

The back jacket photograph is of Walter Dean Myers (right) and his brother George Myers, 1947.

Endpapers: Plate 42, Sections 6 & 7, New York City map series; *p. i:* circa 1929; *pp. ii-iii and p. 15:* photograph by Brown Brothers, c. 1915; *p. 3:* c. 1900; *p. 4:* Winnie Mandela, photograph by Bert Smith, c. 1980; *p. 9:* Black Swan Record label, c. 1920; *p. 10:* 145th Street, photograph by Walter Dean Myers, 1980; *p. 17:* c. 1900; *p. 21:* Lois Smith Keith, c. 1950; *p. 28:* the Reverend Al Sharpton, photograph by Bert Smith, c. 1960; *p. 36:* c. 1940; *p. 38:* c. 1930; *p. 41:* c. 1930; *p. 44:* Dorothy Dandridge, c. 1940; *p. 46:* c. 1910; *p. 51:* c. 1935; *p. 52: Blackbirds of 1928; p. 65:* Strut Flash, c. 1941; *p. 66:* c. 1920; *p. 73: Black Cat Lucky Number Dream Book,* c. 1930; *p. 76:* left *New York Times,* 1946 / right c. 1944; *p. 78:* c. 1944; *p. 80:* c. 1900; *p. 83:* c. 1932; *p. 87:* c. 1940. All of the photographs in this book are from the personal collection of Walter Dean Myers. We apologize for any unintentional omissions and will be pleased to correct any inadvertent errors or omissions in future editions. All Rights Reserved

Text copyright © 2004 by Walter Dean Myers
All Rights Reserved
Printed in the United States of America
www.holidayhouse.com
First Edition
1 3 5 7 9 10 8 6 4 2

Library of Congress Cataloging-in-Publication Data
Myers, Walter Dean, 1937–
    Here in Harlem : poems in many voices / by Walter Dean Myers.—
  1st ed.
     p. cm.
    ISBN 0-8234-1853-7 (hardcover)
    1. African Americans—Poetry. 2. Harlem (New York, N.Y.)—Poetry.
3. Young adult poetry, American. [1. African Americans—Poetry.
2. Harlem (New York, N.Y.)—Poetry. 3. American poetry.] I. Title.
PS3563.Y48H47   2004 811'.54—dc22
2003067605

Contents

Introduction — *viii*

CLARA BROWN'S TESTIMONY ♦ *Part I* — *1*

Mali Evans, 12 ♦ *Student* — 2

Macon R. Allen, 38 ♦ *Deacon* — 5

Henry Johnson, 39 ♦ *Mail Carrier* — 6

Willie Arnold, 30 ♦ *Alto Sax Player* — 8

Terry Smith, 24 ♦ *Unemployed* — 10

CLARA BROWN'S TESTIMONY ♦ *Part II* — *11*

Christopher Lomax, 60 ♦ *Retired* — 12

Junice Lomax, 23 ♦ *Unemployed* — 13

Hosea Liburd, 25 ♦ *Laborer* — 14

William Riley Pitts, 42 ♦ *Jazz Artist* — 16

J. Milton Brooks, 41 ♦ *Undertaker* — 18

John Reese, 70 ♦ *Ballplayer, Janitor* — 19

Eleanor Hayden, 51 ♦ *Nanny* — 20

Tom Fisher, 38 ♦ *Blues Singer, Livery Cabbie* — 22

Dennis Chapman, 40 ♦ *Laborer* — 23

C. C. Castell, 49 ♦ *On Disability* — 26

Reuben Mills, 34 ♦ *Artist*	27
Jimmy Wall, 14 ♦ *Boy Evangelist*	29
John Lee Graham, 49 ♦ *Street Historian*	30
Willie Schockley, 23 ♦ *Street Vendor,*	
Guitar Player	31
Etta Peabody, 60 ♦ *Insurance Adjuster*	33
Delia Pierce, 32 ♦ *Hairdresser*	34
CLARA BROWN'S TESTIMONY ♦ *Part III*	37
Lois Smith, 12 ♦ *Student*	38
Jesse Craig, 38 ♦ *Salesman*	39
Richmond Leake, 53 ♦ *Newsstand Dealer*	40
Helen Sweetland, 27 ♦ *Party Girl*	43
Joshua De Grosse, 19 ♦ *Student, City College*	45
Betty Pointing, 64 ♦ *Clerk*	47
Jonathan Smalls, 29 ♦ *Urban Planner*	48
Adam Crooms, 24 ♦ *Furniture Mover*	50
CLARA BROWN'S TESTIMONY ♦ *Part IV*	53
Malcolm Jones, 16 ♦ *Student*	54
Gerry Jones, 14 ♦ *Student*	55
Mary Ann Robinson, 30 ♦ *Nurse,*	
Harlem Hospital	56
Ann Carter, 32 / Benjamin Bailey, 38 ♦	
Switchboard Operator / Building Maintenance	57
Ernest Scott, 26 ♦ *Poet*	58

Caroline Fleming, 42 ♦ *Live-in Maid*	59
Effie Black, 58 ♦ *Church Organist*	60
Marcia Williams, 17 ♦ *High School Senior*	61
Harland Keith, 33 ♦ *Reporter*	62
Lawrence Hamm, 19 ♦ *Student Athlete*	63
Sam DuPree, 28 ♦ *Hustler*	64
CLARA BROWN'S TESTIMONY ♦ *Part V*	67
Didi Taylor, 14 ♦ *Student*	68
Dana Greene, 18 ♦ *Education Major, City College*	69
Bill Cash, 30 ♦ *Boxer*	70
William Dandridge, 67 ♦ *Mechanic*	71
Charles Biner, 57 ♦ *Composer, X-Ray Technician*	72
John Brambles, 55 ♦ *Numbers Runner*	73
Homer Grimes, 83 ♦ *Blind Veteran*	75
Frank Griffin, 82 ♦ *Veteran*	76
Lemuel Burr, 81 ♦ *Veteran*	77
CLARA BROWN'S TESTIMONY ♦ *Part VI*	81
Lydia Cruz, 15 ♦ *Student*	82
Kevin Broderick, 20 ♦ *Pre-Law, City College*	84
Earl Prentiss, 39 ♦ *Motorman*	85
Clara Brown, 87 ♦ *Retired*	87
Some people, places, and terms . . .	88

Introduction

When I was in high school, I first read Edgar Lee Masters's book of poems *Spoon River Anthology*. The idea of creating a fictional town and people (buried in the fictional Spoon River cemetery) intrigued me. As the idea for this book ripened in my mind, I began to imagine a street corner in Harlem, the Harlem of my youth, and the very much alive people who would pass that corner. So began *Here in Harlem*.

The characters in this book all represent people I have known or whose lives have touched mine. I vividly remember the story of the World War II veteran who was blinded by a southern sheriff. I remember too when my Bible school class visited St. Joseph's and an old black man who came with us wondered why the mass (then said in Latin) was so quiet. He loved "a shouting church." I loved him.

So many of my heroes are in this book. Langston Hughes used to do readings and sell his books from a shopping bag in my church. Countee Cullen taught school a few blocks from my house. Joe Louis had the good grace to shake his huge fist at the kids on my block. Other residents have become heroes to me. The nurse working at Harlem Hospital, the old men sitting on Lenox Avenue, the brilliant black children dancing through the streets of my sweet village. The poets, the lovers, the musicians, and those who sweat from day to day just to survive.

I have added photographs to the text because I love the images, not to match the poems. The images and the voices race through my mind in a sustained triumph of place and community.

I have written a poem that is an unabashed tribute to the poet W. B. Yeats, in homage to his advice to playwright John Millington Synge. He told Synge to write about a community that he could truly love, whose people would gladden his heart. For Synge it was the Aran Islands, for me it is Harlem.

Clara Brown's Testimony

Part I

Everybody's asking me why I'm always talking about Harlem. Well, child, to me, Harlem is like an old friend. Sometimes she won't do right, or do exactly what you want her to do. Sometimes she's needy when you don't have anything extra to be giving. But you know what to expect from a real friend, and that's what Harlem has been to me.

And if you give to Harlem, it always finds a way to give back. When I hear music coming from the apartment windows or from the doors of a storefront church, I know that's Harlem giving me a gift. And it's music that's more than just head music. It's music my soul remembers from way past what my brain knows about.

I love the people of Harlem, too. Yes, that's right, all of them. Because one by one they may not be that much. But, honey, all together, they're Harlem, and you can't ask for more than that.

Mali Evans, 12
Student

I'd like to be old one day
Like Mrs. Purvis with her gray
Hair like a halo around her black face
She says it's her crown, her tiara
She walks slowly, grandly
Down the avenue, as if the streets
Were her queendom and even
The winos smile and bow
Or raise their hands in greeting
I would like to be an ancient lady
Tree-tough and deep-rooted
In the rich soil of my dark
Foreverness
And the only thing white I would wear
Is the crown about my
Sweet black face

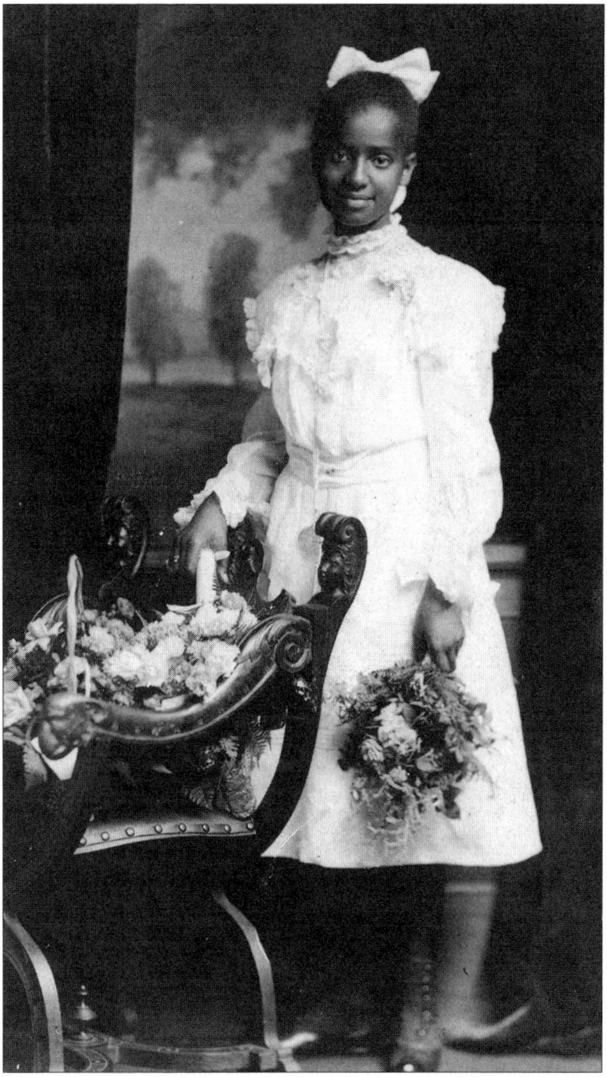

4

Macon R. Allen, 38
Deacon

I love a shouting church!
Praises bounding off the ceiling
The rhythm catching up the feet
Tambourines that send the spirits reeling
    Yes, give me a shouting church!
    A big sister wiping at her face
    Praising Jesus to a jump-up preacher
    As he hollers gospel on the way to grace
Lord, give me a shouting church!
Where everybody knows the end is coming fast
And the righteous speak in tongues
Saying, "Sinner, don't let this harvest pass"
    Don't give me no whispering church
    Don't be mumbling nothing to my Lord
    You came in crying and you going out crying
    So don't be holding back the word
Oh, Lord, I love a shouting church!
Wake up Lazarus! Wake up Paul!
Wake the congregation, and lift their hearts
If they don't hear it now, they won't hear at all
Oh, I love a shouting church!
Can I get an A-men?

Henry Johnson, 39
Mail Carrier

Sitting inside Ray's Barbershop
Looking across the avenue
I saw
A little black man
Sweat staining his underarms
Glistening on his brow
Fists pumping up the fire
Of the noontime air
Sweet cullud voice
Soft as Sunday cotton
Hard as Monday cropping
Under a hell-hot Georgia sun
    Could be Marcus, I said
    Could be Martin, came a voice from down
        the way
    Sounds like Malcolm, rang from the shadows

Sitting inside Sylvia's
I saw
A tall black man
    Singing about revolution
    And how the gentrified evolution
    Has brought about the devolution
Of Songhai, Mali, and Timbuktu
    Grinning instead of winning
    Chicken instead of stickin'

To a righteous path
    Could be Marcus, I said
    Could be Martin, came a voice from down
        the way
    Sounds like Malcolm, rang from the shadows

Sitting inside the Victory Temple Church
Of God in Christ
    I saw a black man rocking
    Preaching and teaching
    Calling for the congregation
    To bring forth a mighty nation
That would be free at last
That would put aside the blasphemous
    Sin of compromise
    Keep their eyes on the prize
And their minds on bizness
    Could be Marcus, I said
    Could be Martin, came a voice from down
        the way
    Sounds like Malcolm, rang from the shadows

Willie Arnold, 30
Alto Sax Player

"He bops!"

That's what they're saying
When I'm playing
When I'm wailing
Hot notes sailing
Like soulful birds
Songs without words

"Be-bop!"

The joint is swinging
Hearts are singing
As I'm blowing
Really flowing
Up to the moon
With this sweet tune

He bops!
She bops!
We bop!
Be bop!

My horn will free you
Or maybe freeze you
In some rhapsodic frieze

It's a swinging rap
To wrap around your brain
A jazzy feat
You'll pat your feet
To this refrain
What can I say?

I can say
Be-bop!
Be-bop bo dee and
Be-bop!
Be-bop bo dee and
Be-bop
Be-bop a bo
Deee!

"He bops!"

That's what they're saying
When I'm playing
When I'm wailing
Hot notes sailing
Like soulful birds
Songs without words

Last call
That's all!

Terry Smith, 24
Unemployed

The hiss of the stove is soft
As soft as the gentle snowfall
That fills the street below
Christmas carols rise from the alley
And I feel the child moving against my side
His crying, hoarse after the first minutes,
Has stopped and his breath
Is like a sigh against my breast
Christmas
The last straw crumbled weeks ago
The last man happened years before
The last hope tiptoed past the door
And the holidays are here again
Breathe deeply, child
The Magi have gone another way

Clara Brown's Testimony

Part II

The first time my heart was broken, it was by the Cotton Club. I was too young and full of myself for no boy to hurt me. Me and my sister, Vicky, heard they were having tryouts for the chorus line. We could both dance, and we practiced our little routine until it was right. We called ourselves the Queen Sisters. I don't know why— we just thought it fit us.

When it was time for us to show our stuff, we did it with style! You hear me? I knew we were good when we walked in the door. The woman picking the dancers said she would let us know, and I made sure she had our right address.

We changed into our street clothes and was just about ready to leave when the piano player stopped us. "I'm sorry, girls. You were good," he said. "But they only hire light-skinned girls to dance here."

I couldn't tell you what that man looked like today. You ever try to look at somebody with tears in your eyes and your lip quivering so bad you can't talk? That was the day I learned that being black wasn't no simple thing, even in Harlem.

Christopher Lomax, 60
Retired

I see my daughter
Her beauty lies across the moment
Like the sun, already dipped
Below the horizon,
Caresses the darkened ripples of a lake

Leaning against the light
Pole she nods, half tired
Half benumbed
Her body bobs and jerks
A puppet on a rubber band
A willow in the memory
Of a storm

This is what I have planted
This sap-poisoned flower
This anguished goddess of the boulevard
Thorned, her black fern fingers
Scratch idly at her face
As I wipe the tears from mine
I drop my head
My feet shuffle away from my heart
Toward my heart
Toward my brown angel, fallen from grace
Traffic, chromed and blurred with color
Passes between us and she is gone
A mirage of pain

Junice Lomax, 23
Unemployed

I see my father
Hurt lines etched deeply
In his mahogany face
Like an ancient map of pain
His dark eyes are tired
Having seen too much, known too much
Struggled too much to turn away
And have not turned away
For a wild moment
Our glances meet
Like lambs in the whirlwind
And I am his lost child again
And his forgiving heart reaches
Across the busy avenue
Too late
We are chasmed by the blurring crowd
I hear him calling from below
As I race recklessly across
A thousand frantic highs

Hosea Liburd, 25
Laborer

When the doors close and the A train begins
Its rock/jerk journey downtown
I am diminished, made small
My manhood left, abandoned, on the station
    platform
Under the 125 sign
When the doors part and the A train sucks in
The nervous close/clutched horde
Their fear-wide eyes ablaze
With quiet cautions
I become the beast
And huge in my beastness
I and they look away
Each praying invisibility
Me thinking of a package left abandoned
On the station platform
Under the 125 sign

APARTMENTS TO LET.
3 or 4 Rooms with Improvements
For Respectable Colored Families Only.
BERNHEIMER & SCHWARTZ
PILSENER
BREWG CO.
BEERS
FAMILY ENTRANCE

William Riley Pitts, 42
Jazz Artist

Sometimes, I sit and wonder
What the boy could have been
That's how he plays in my mind: the boy
Not Bill Jr. or son
My tongue can't find the right words to sing of him
    That night
    When her blues/scream didn't tear down
    The world
    Didn't make it right again
    His mother hid away
    In the dark corners of her soul
    And turned her heart so it read closed on
    Both sides
I thought there was a distance
Beyond the mourning, some little space
To move toward
Some saving chord
Some wild and desperate chorus
Leading to a redemptive coda
But it all comes back to a 4/4
Knock on the door and a policeman
Uneasy in his stretched humanity
Stumbling through a riff that was all notes
And no rhythm, no rhyme
Saying there had been an accident

I push my horn into a cab
Hustle to another gig, another stand
Another mike. I push the brassy growl
Of my dead tongue
Through predictable changes

As I play I wonder about the boy
And the melody he took with him

J. Milton Brooks, 41
Undertaker

Dying is not an easy trip, no matter what they say
The night ahead is long and how short was the day
I've carried these boxes, wheeled them down the aisle
And drove them slow past the Apollo for that last mile
For some it's all tears and bitter grief
Others are tired and glad of the relief
I try to move it along, try to ease the pain
I tell the kin, it's just the tired body lain
On satin sheets, faces powdered, hair combed
They lie there sleeping, they'll wake up home
But there comes a time when I have to weep
It's when we lay some teenage boy so deep
I close my eyes and pray the Lord to save
Me from watching old men shuffling children to the grave

John Reese, 70
Ballplayer, Janitor

When only the ball was white
We played doubleheaders in Pelican Park and
Rickwood Stadium on sultry Sunday
Afternoons and loved every swinging
Bat, every blurred pitch screaming
Into the dark pop of a catcher's mitt
Every after-church voice, Negro black against
The amber bleachers as we ran/strained/lunged
Through the swirling dust of our youth

We were roaring eagles, the barons of our
Turf, monarchs ruling a joyful world
Then Jackie broke through/stomped through
Tore down the gates that had held us back
He was our hero, Ajax in triumph, as the
Crowds cheered on

But when the dust had settled to the ground
And when the cheers had faded into the distance
All that was left was the silence of our
Empty stadiums

The silence and the memories of the glory that had
  been
On sultry Sunday afternoons

Eleanor Hayden, 51
Nanny

My ankles were aching with shooting pains
All up in my joints and I was weary, soaked
Down to the bone! Down to the very bone!
But there I was shuffling off the A train
Ringing the white folks' bell—"How are you,
    ma'am?"
And "Yes, I know I should get here before seven
'Cause you got that important job downtown
To go to. And I know you want me to take Tiffany to
Central Park early before the sun gets too hot.
    Uh-huh."
She spit out a word and sealed it with a sneer
And a slam of the door to show just how mad she was
Course she would have really been mad
Seeing me and Little Miss Ann swinging
Our fine selves into the Apollo Theater
Or eating curried meat pies on Lenox Avenue
And how I hope I'm around when her sweet
Little white child comes out with her first blues!
I'm going to say she got it from the television

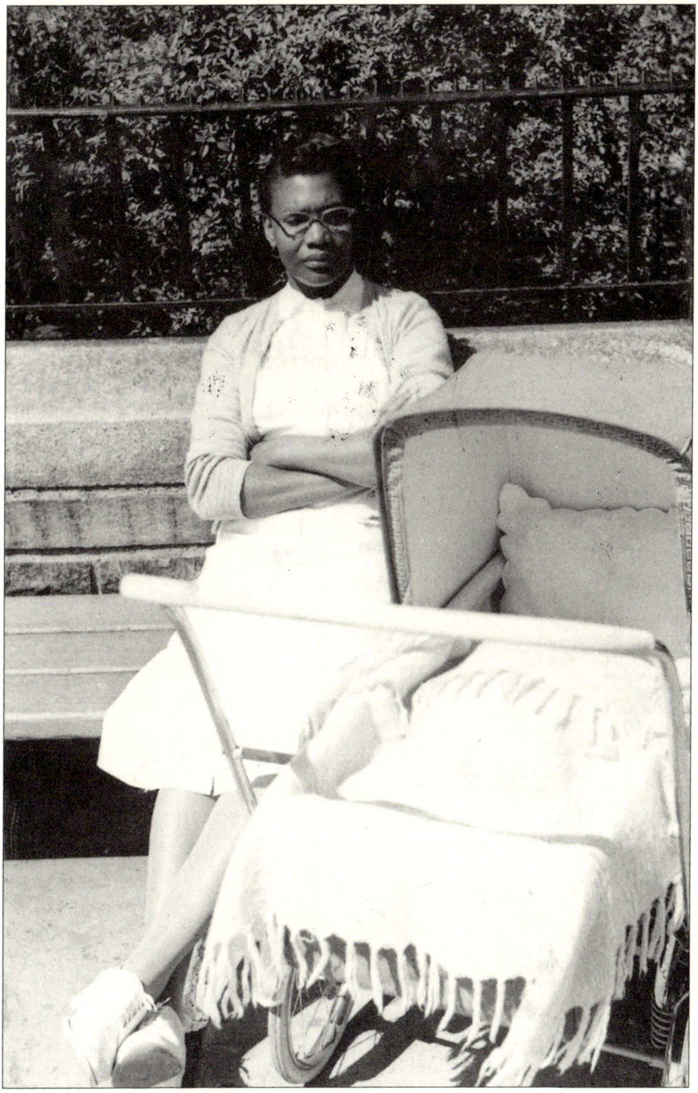

Tom Fisher, 38
Blues Singer, Livery Cabbie

I got a fat Georgia woman, Sweet Martha is her name
I got a fat Georgia woman, Sweet Martha is her name
She's mean and she's ornery, but I loves her all the same

She's a coal black woman, she walk so nice and loose
She's a coal black woman, she walk so nice and loose
She's darker than the berry, sweeter than the juice

I wandered up to Paris, made my way to Rome
I wandered up to Paris, made my way to Rome
Ran out of money, Martha said, "C'mon home"

When I pass on to glory, don't want no starry crown
When I passes on to glory, don't want no starry crown
Just find my Sweet Martha, lay my tired body down

Dennis Chapman, 40
Laborer

I had a piece of land down south
A square patch near where the creek
Muddy and sullen, turned like the crook
Of a finger, pointing innocently eastward
But I was drunk with bright/light dreams
The electric kaleidoscope of boundless freedom
And so I flew, I flew
Leaving my crop behind, sugar beets in the field
And a soft-angled woman who watched
As my silhouette lessened to a speck
On the far horizon
Harlem blared a welcome—flashed its smile
Rolled its city eyes, blew out its dark city breath

Nibbled hungrily at my liver as I
Lived it up and boogied down
Ran it up, and spun it round
Harlem eased me, calmed me, rubbed my chest
Held me close on restless nights
Whispered in my ear that the blues loved only me
And that it was joy, not despair, that spread
Like sunrise
On the far horizon
Now the prison of my skin is cold, and damp
As I push a stub of pencil across the card

Now the peeling yellowed walls lean in
To read my stumbling words, my truths

Won't you come up, please? I beg
You won't like being crowded, or the noise
There are more corners in my small room
Than in all of Alabama. . . .
But there's a song here, or is it a moan?
And an excitement that floats
In the heavy air
We pat our feet to bring it groundward
All that, and
A broken neon bird that flaps its wing
On the far horizon
No winters are as cold as city-cold
And my cracked life/being leaks badly in the chill
    of rain
The hope I've stuffed around the edges
Of my days fell out last season
And the dreams in the window box
Died with early frost
But there's a life here that whirls
Along the curbs
Lifting, breeze caught, eddy driven
Too fast for me to catch and hold
It's all I have to offer
Except that I need you
To fill the spaces in the broken mirror
Of who I am

I hope this letter finds you well
Finds you

By the time the Greyhound bus had stopped
Had let the soft-angled woman off with her case
Had loosed her in the city, she had grayed
The angles harder, the gaze distant
"How did you leave the crops?" I asked.
"Dead," she answered, her voice weary, flat. "Any
    chance of a new growth in the spring?"
    I asked.
"I'm here," she said. "Show me the fields."
Her eyes already looking beyond me, already
On the far horizon

C. C. Castell, 49
On Disability

The difference between here in Harlem
And Mississippi where I come from
Is that here the young peoples is in a hurry
To get somewhere even if they don't
Know rightly where they in a hurry to get to
And that's okay because it means they
Think they important enough to get something
Done and whatever little thing they trying to
Get done is going to mean something to
Somebody so's they in a hurry to do that little
Thing. Now I been sitting here on this stoop
Most of the time, more or less, and I ain't doing
Nothing and I ain't in a hurry to get nowhere
But I enjoys watching the young folk
Because even if one or two of them is right, see,
Well, that's what you calls
Progress

Reuben Mills, 34
Artist

Vein red, bruise purple
The pallet of my soul drips slowly
Onto the canvas of this life

Flashing amber, blinding white
Garish hues screaming through the night
Orange reflections on a switchblade knife

Undertaker gray, church-organ gold
Moonlight glimmer against mahogany
A moiré pattern edged in strife

Moody midnight shadings of the blues
Pink raised welt on an amber back
A rich tapestry of muted hues
All to create the pointillist color of black

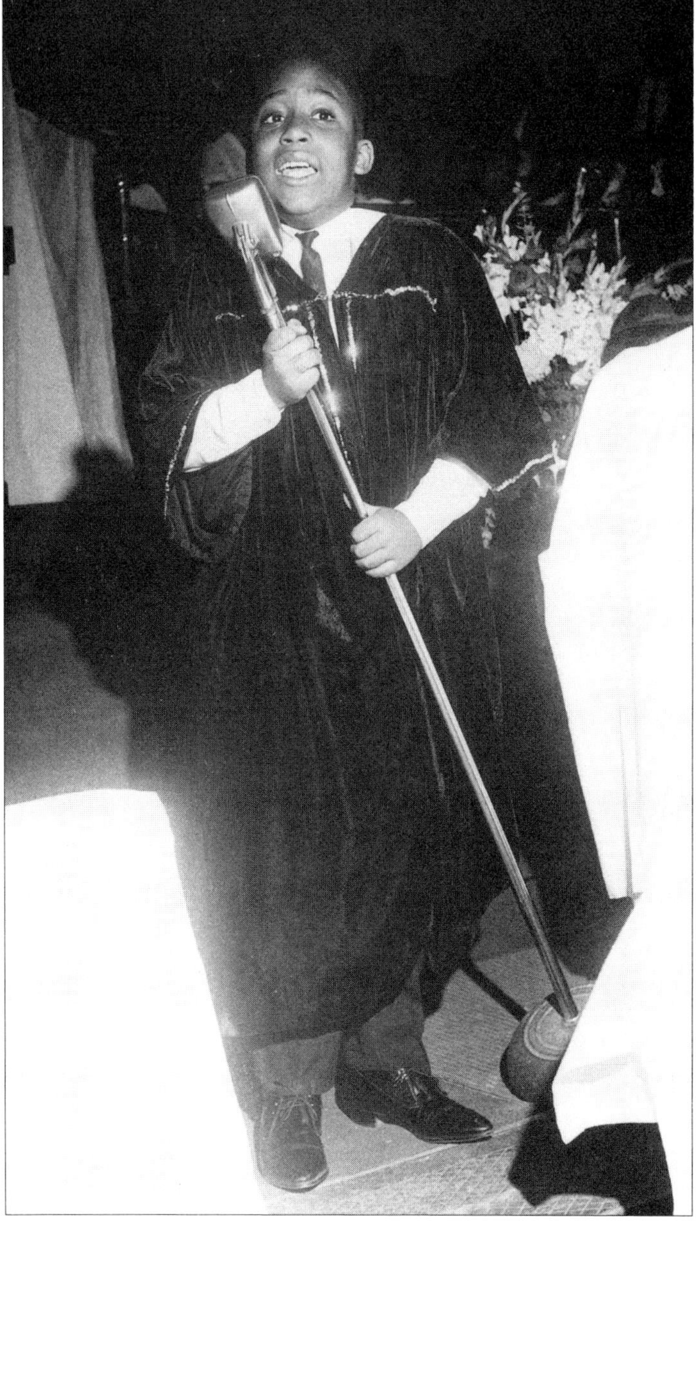

Jimmy Wall, 14
Boy Evangelist

Green shoots pushing through
The cracked concrete pavement
Have faith in sun and sky
And hope for God
As they proclaim the ecstasy of rosedom
From the redbrick tenements
My warrior angel tongue
Roaring fury
No longer through a glass darkly
But with the clarity of I am
And I love
I proclaim
I am a man

John Lee Graham, 49
Street Historian

I have captured the moment
When an Igbo child watched the play of sunlight
Across his fingers
On the banks of the Ogun

I have captured the moment
When a Bantu herdsman squatted silently
To contemplate the beauty of his woman
In the steamy Kalahari

I have captured the moment
When a Kikuyu woman smiled
As she held a moment of silence in her bosom
At the foot of Mount Kenya

I have captured the moment
When the victorious Songhai warriors
Triumphantly sang the songs of the elders
At the bend of the Niger

I have captured the moment
When the scholars of Timbuktu
And the sages of Harlem flew together
In lazy circles over the broad Atlantic

Strong grows the rising heart
Stronger still the deepening mind

Willie Schockley, 23
Street Vendor, Guitar Player

I got home the other morning
I guess it was about half past two
Found my clothes lying on the sidewalk
And my picture torn in two
I think she trying to tell me something
I think my baby is trying to tell me something
About those lay-down Harlem blues

I got down on my knees
There were tears rolling from my eyes
She said, "Willie, don't say a word
'Cause I'm tired of listening to your lies."
I think she trying to tell me something
I think my baby is trying to tell me something
About those lay-down Harlem blues

I said, "Baby, baby, baby
Give your Willie just one more chance
I'm gonna give you all my money
And fill your life with sweet romance
Yes, I am
And you know I can do it, Mama."

She said, "No way, no way, no way
You did me wrong from the very start
You need to find you another home
While I try to mend this broken heart

Go on, now
Don't even say good-bye
Don't even say good-bye."

I used to skip and run like lightning
You could call me a playing fool
But she turned me out and closed the door
And now I'm in heartbreak school
I think she trying to tell me something
I think my baby is trying to tell me something
About those lay-down Harlem blues

Etta Peabody, 60
Insurance Adjuster

They told us we had to sit in the "Colored" section
At the Alhambra Theater
And we marched proudly up them stairs
Grinning and carrying on and
Rooting for Errol Flynn and talking back
Like old Errol knew we were watching
From Nigger Heaven

Well, all the noise we made got the
White folks so upset we couldn't
Go back to that movie
And we had to go crosstown to the Sunset
And watch Harlem on the Range
And Hopalong Cassidy and that was
All right, too

'Cause we didn't mind being with each other
And liking each other—"Walk together, children,"
The old folks used to say—
But us walking together and talking
Together just got the white folks even madder
And they closed the colored theater
And put us back in Heaven

Delia Pierce, 32
Hairdresser

It's not like me to run my mouth
But when Darlene says she's going south
I'm wondering who she's going south to see
'Cause her mama lives on 116th Street over the
    Busy Bee
That's that little jazz place that's open all night
And it's so dark in there they must be doing
    something that ain't right

Any-way . . .
Did you hear that Carla's getting married
That's what I heard
The second? This is at least her third
She uses men like a Christmas tree uses tinsel
When she writes her married name, she always uses
    pencil
You talking about exes, that woman got a stack
And I could say something about them
But I'm not the kind to talk behind nobody's back

Any-way . . .
Sister Smith came in yesterday
Said she wanted her hair in curls
Meanwhile that no-good man of hers
Is running with those project girls
Yes, he is, and they can't be but half his age

She should throw the book at him, page by page
And she ain't no saint, with all her righteous ways
That old heifer has had some shady days

Any-way . . .
The word's going around on Cindy Lou
I knew she was too good to be true
Ain't nobody know for sure but you see that smile
That girl knows more than her prayers and it's just her style
To be sneaking out late and playing like she's young
On the social ladder she's under the bottom rung

Any-way . . .
Betty Mae came in, yes, that old fat tub
You know she says she used to dance at the Cotton Club
And she used to wear fine lace and diamonds galore
That must have been just before the Civil War
When that slab of bacon slid off the rack
And Deacon Grier popped in the other day
You know if he could have his way
He'd sit home all day and sip champagne
With that light-skinned chick they call Baby Jane
There's a lot of people around here who are kinda slack
But you know I ain't the kind to talk behind nobody's back

Miss Patty said I should tell his wife
But I wouldn't do that to save my life
Only person who would be that mean
Is Miss Fake Nails herself, uh-huh, Darlene
She's down south now, supposed to be working on
    her tan
Ask me she trying to sniff her out a man
But my mouth is sealed, you don't even see a crack
'Cause I ain't the kind to talk behind nobody's back

Clara Brown's Testimony

Part III

Mama was getting old, and she was so happy 'cause she thought I had found God at Abyssinian Baptist. I was singing four nights a week at the Showcase Lounge, down from the Apollo, and she didn't know just what I was finding there. God had always been good to me, but I didn't want to tell Mama that I had joined Abyssinian because I wanted to sing in their choir. This old long-headed boy named Nathan—used to put cocoa butter on his skin, and you could smell it when he got close—said God wanted me to sing in church because that was my true calling. I thought any time I sang my heart out, I was praising God.

One time I was singing so good on a Sunday morning, Nathan asked me what I was so happy about. I told him I was happy that the Dodgers got them a colored baseball player. He said I shouldn't be getting happy over color.

I guess it was wrong to tell him to shut his fool self up on Easter Sunday, but I did.

Lois Smith, 12
Student

One day I'd like a school named after me
And all the kids would wonder, "Who was she?"
They'd probably think I was some rich white lady
And not someone cute and a little shady
Then one day they'd find me in a book
Check out my name and take a second look
Then I'd be as famous as old Booker T.
And young kids would want to grow up to be like me

Jesse Craig, 38
Salesman

I knew Langston
Laughed with the man

In West Harlem
With me thinking

This is no Keats
No fair Shelley

This is Negro
Quintessential

Rice and collards
Down-home brother

He knew rivers
And rent-due blues

And what it meant
To poet Black

Richmond Leake, 53
Newsstand Dealer

Teachers did not listen
When I was young
They had things to tell
Lessons to teach and
Papers to grade
So I just shut up

I married young but
She was too busy to
Hear me, what with
Her planning for a
Better life, for the future
And things she had to get done

The white man I
Worked for had all
He could do making money and
Making sure I wasn't
Stealing
Sometimes, though he
Nodded
On his way out the door
And I nodded back

I prayed a lot, for
A raise, for the rent when I needed it,

Cigarettes
18¢
BLACKEY
BEANS
GRANGER
RUSSELL'S
QUAKER
MOUNDS
Ridley's
Dr. I.Q.
5¢

But nothing ever came
Without a kick
And I thought God
Must have been
Listening to folks in India

Now I talk to myself a
Lot and people worry
That I'm not in touch
But they're wrong because
What moves me is when I
Talk I listen
And when I asks a question
I answer
Ain't nothing wrong with that

Helen Sweetland, 27
Party Girl

Oh, swing that swing
Sing the song you need to sing
Don't hold back, Jack
And don't give no slack
It's time to par-tee
There was a time of taffeta and dreams
Of cozy warm imaginings
Bright meteors spinning
Along rainbow beams
Through an endless universe
Oh, swing that swing
Sing the song you need to sing
Don't hold back, Jack
And don't give no slack
It's time to par-tee

There was a time of gentle peeling
The pirouette of tiny feet
Away from the innocence, the sweet
Dance, the delicious feeling
As hope and promise merge
Oh, swing that swing
Sing the song you need to sing
Don't hold back, Jack
And don't give no slack
It's time to par-tee

There was a time of eddy and swirl
Too many days that would not start
Nights of nervous nibbling on the heart
The angel's fall to party girl
While no one in heaven wept
Oh, swing that swing
Sing the song you need to sing
Don't hold back, Jack
And don't give no slack
It's time to par-teeee

Joshua De Grosse, 19
Student, City College

I cannot write of beauty with this blind pen.
These gnarled fingers are useless things.
Scratchy useless syllables again and again.
Cairo cries; the raged word wings.

I am too big, too hard, too gross to feel,
Too poor of soul to write of queens and kings.
My neighbor's despair, that's what's real.
Cairo cries; the raged word wings.

There is no tenderness in my sweaty nights,
No sweet ethereal happenings
To rhyme, no startle of northern lights.
Cairo cries; the raged word wings.

For me there are no seagulls swooping wine-dark
    seas,
No angel child who oh-so-sweetly sings,
No magic moment for my poet's tongue to seize.
Cairo cries; the raged word wings.

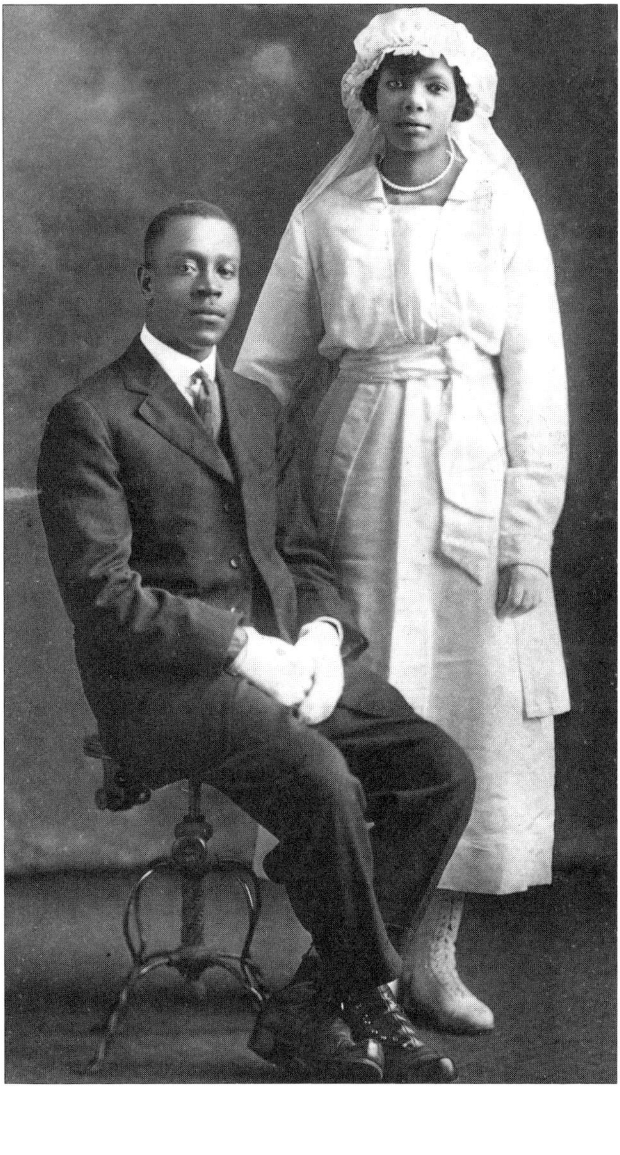

Betty Pointing, 64
Clerk

He asked me why I smile when I say "I love you."
I don't know why I smile—I just do. He said I
shouldn't smile when I say it because then he don't
think I'm serious. I've been with him forty-six years
and I told him that should stand for something, but
he still said I shouldn't smile when I say I love him.
So I got myself all tighted up and looked him right
in his face and said "I love you," but no sooner
than the "I" was halfway out, I was smiling again.
I just can't help smiling when I say it. I truly can't.
I smiled the first time I ever seen that man standing
in the back of the church trying to ease out before
the service was over. Even when he ain't around
sometimes I find myself thinking on him and
smiling. So now I'm standing in front of the mirror
feeling like a fool saying "I love you" to myself for
practice so when he comes home from the barbershop
I can say it to him. And I know, same as I know my
name, that when I open my mouth to say it to his
face, I'm going to be smiling. Shoot, he know it, too.

Jonathan Smalls, 29
Urban Planner

In the crazy quilt patterns of the city
Stretched taut in the balmy
Summer wind
There are more reds than yellows
More browns than reds
And black everywhere

Between the huddled buildings
Tiny rectangles of gray-blue sky
Signal that there is a
Beyond
While above the rooftops
The horizon, cut into sharp shapes
Antenna tweaked, its definition
Lost to the belching tenement smoke,
Is diminished
The redbrick squares
Chipped with history
Speak in a complex tongue
Complete with clicks and chords and that
Peculiar staccato chirping rising
From the anti-frantic sidewalks
Below

The colors of Harlem frieze
And unfreeze into a thousand

Fluid landscapes
The artists are the colors
The colors are the art
More reds than yellows
More browns than red
And black everywhere

Adam Crooms, 24
Furniture Mover

The rent party's
Get-in quarter
Took me upstairs
To the laughter.

The off rhythm
Of tinkling glass
Caught the high laugh
Of a sweet thing

Pinning it fast
Against the wall
While all the time
Johnson's left hand

Swept the bass keys
In that mean stride
He could bring up
From somewhere deep

Inside his black
Mississippi
Hunched-over frame
And yellow nails.

We forgot rent
Scoffed at Monday
Turned worry loose
And put it out

"You watching me?"
Johnson just grinned
While that big hand
Scratched God's broad back.

I CAN'T GIVE YOU ANYTHING BUT LOVE
(BABY)
LEW LESLIE'S
BLACKBIRDS
of
1928
with
UKULELE
ARRANGEMENT
I CAN'T GIVE YOU ANYTHING BUT LOVE
I MUST HAVE THAT MAN
DIG A DIG A DO
DOIN' THE NEW LOW-DOWN
SHUFFLE YOUR FEET AND ROLL ALONG
BANDANNA BABIES
HERE COMES MY BLACKBIRD
DIXIE
Lyrics by
DOROTHY FIELDS
Music by
JIMMY McHUGH
LEFF
JACK MILLS INC.
Music Publishers
MADE IN U.S.A.

Clara Brown's Testimony

Part IV

I lived in fancy places on Morningside Avenue and some little dinky places around the neighborhood. Once I had a little room on 132nd Street right over that church that used to be a theater. Room was just about big enough to change your mind in, and it had a mouse that lived in it what would come out any time I played a Duke Ellington record. I told my sister, Vicky, about that mouse and she asked me, "What do a mouse know about jazz?"

I told her I didn't know what he knew about jazz, but I knew he had some good taste in music. Then her boyfriend, a slick-haired boy with bad teeth, came by and put on an old shake-your-booty blues tune. That mouse came right out his hole, strolled big as you please across the linoleum, and went behind the refrigerator. Vicky said, "I thought he just liked the Duke!" and laughed.

I think that mouse just did that to irk me.

Malcolm James, 16
Student

*"So what are you going to do with your life?"
Aunt Ginny asked.*

Do? Do?
Perhaps I'll put it in a Mason jar
It would fit on the shelf
Next to Grandpa's leather pouch
Still reeking with tobacco smells from
A hundred years ago
Or next to the faded picture
Of the woman they say
Was in our family though her
Skin was lighter than anyone
Else's and where would she get a name like
Louvenia scrawled on the back
Or maybe I will put my life in the
Drawer next to my dead father's
National Maritime Union card
And be as proud of it as he was of that
Tattered rectangle

Gerry Jones, 14
Student

From my fire escape tower
I watch the whirl and swirl
Of the dance below
My hearts, Mya and June Girl, wave up to me
The smells of collard greens and curried chicken
Drifting from the kitchen
Warm-edge my thoughts
As I sit cross-legged, anchored by my
Book of poems
Inside, Bible anchored
Under the cast-iron lamp, its globe
Like some private sun
Grandma sits and rocks
Down the street a car squeals to a halt
I look up, a bare-chested, gold-toothed brother
Shakes his fist
At a slow-strutting sultry sister whose hips
Shake her answer
Seeing there is no need for Royal Intervention
I turn the page

Mary Ann Robinson, 30
Nurse, Harlem Hospital

Eyes desperation-bright or despair-flat
They come in a steady stream
To be handled by strangers as Death
Spins the hands of the clock
Not quite centered on the not quite
Yellow walls
They come together, lust and laughter
Reduced to gasp and gurgle
To pipes and tubes, digital numbers
Flickering on a dark screen, mocking, threatening
To disappear beyond the edge of the universe
Then, when the night of vacant stares, of prayers
Of crying,
Then, when the night of miracles and casual dying,
Is ended,
And dawn streaks like heaven's wound across
The rooftops,
I punch out and start my walk to home,
down 135th Street
I pause to watch the morning children's games
Neighbors gathering before they leave the Village
To go downtown, while all the while
I think of the clock on the not quite yellow wall

Ann Carter, 32 / Benjamin Bailey, 38
Switchboard Operator / Building Maintenance

"I saw JEEESUS yesterday."
    "No, you didn't, no way."
"He was wearing a white robe and sandals."
    "This hot sun is more than you can handle."
"I said, 'Welcome to Harlem, Lord.'"
    "Maybe you ain't crazy—maybe you're just bored."
"He said, 'Sister Carter, you're looking well!'"
    "If I believed in roots, I'd figure you for a spell!"
"Then I said, 'O, Lord, I hope I haven't died!'"
    "I'm going past the crazy house—you need a ride?"
"JEEESUS said He just come to play the drums!"
    "Yeah, and Rockefeller come to see the slums!"
"I said, 'Thou will do what Thou will do!'"
    "And he was willing to talk to you?"
"JEEESUS hailed a cab and said, 'So long!'"
    "Now, Sister Carter, you know you wrong!"
"I saw JEEESUS yesterday."
    "No, you didn't, girl, no way!"
"I saw Mooooses, just this morning!"
    "You saw who???"
"I saw Mooooses, just this morning!"
    "That's it, sister—I'm through!"

Ernest Scott, 26
Poet

I stood on the tree of life
Mouth gaped wide
Sucking in the music of the crosstown breeze
When I had filled my lungs near bursting (Cullen,
    Hughes, Hurston)
I began my song, a black melody
Gathered from the several seas
Warmed by the mistral winds
Rhythmed by the slapping Congo tide

I stood tall on the tree of life
Rapt with wonder
Listening to the resonance of the project walls
I claimed ownership of the joyful noise (Baldwin,
    Wright, Du Bois)
I was the chorus, the doo-wop from dim halls
My words fogged the neon night
My rhymes tamed the thunder

Caroline Fleming, 42
Live-in Maid

Now and then
After a day of smiling too hard
Or a day of holding back
The tears too long
And I am caught arrow tight
With nerves screeching like talons
Grating slowly across concrete
When my throat is numb with unspeaking
And my inner voice is too small to
Reach God's ears
I long for my people

Now and then
When the pills don't touch the pain
And chairs don't ease the weariness
Of loving someone else's child
Too much, and carefully
Arranging someone else's
Tattered life
When Thursday is an eternity
Away and I am too old
For eternities
I long for my people

Effie Black, 58
Church Organist

You have to start with a tuned ear
To pick out the notes, and all the sounds between
And you have to open up and really hear
The street songs and what those sounds mean
To the strollers and the sitters on the steps
Looking as if they're moving a bit but all the while
The sounds are coming out of them as well
And every once in a while a foot would pat
And a hand would shake, a finger snap
You have to hear how those chords are built
How an ebbing fifth covers a silent third
In a way that gets between the bone and flesh
And how all those perfect harmonies
Echo the sweet voice of a living God

Marcia Williams, 17
High School Senior

He spread his nets along
The broad expanse of a smile
So brilliant I thought it was
The full moon, silver, pregnant
Above the gentle waves
And all the time pretending not to see me
Splashing warily
Just beyond the breakers
I dared him
Knowing I was stronger than neap and high
Slyer than dolphins, ready to deny
The dazzle of bait, believing
That chum would never lead beyond
Itself even as I floated
Along the foamy edges of gravity
Seaweed in my hair
And all the familiar dangers of fisherman
And sea creature stirring
In my swimmer's heart and in the siren song
Reverberating from love's dark
Uncertain shore

Harland Keith, 33
Reporter

There are beasts in the far
Corners of my mind
They crouch, prepared to spring
From the shadows
Ready to pounce, to leap
Screaming their curses
Fangs bared, eager to
Suck the whiteness from my bones

There are beasts in the far
Corners of my mind
They call to me
"Black man, black man, it is warm
Here in the lonely exile of your dead history
Come lie with us, come sleep. Come sleep."
I put aside my gentle verses
My haunted dreams
I learn to love the darkness

Lawrence Hamm, 19
Student Athlete

It's more than the ball—
Blur dribbled down the hardwood floor—
More than the step past you,
Greater than the lift, the awesome soar
Through space, rim high, higher,
And the monster jam that crumbles
Egos, all this and moves
So sweet they make shadows stumble.
I own this sacred space
This holy court, these painted lanes
The kiss of palm on glass
These kicks, the smell of sweat and pain.
Call me muscle, and flight.
"Gone!" is my name, and "Slam!"
In this sweet universe
Of Ball, I am! I am!

Sam DuPree, 28
Hustler

Sweet Sam DuPree
Some people break, some people bend
Some just fade away, others go looking for a friend
With a shoulder they can cry on
Or a few dollars they can rely on
They go low ride gliding
Or ducking or hiding
Spend all day looking down at their feet
'Cause they're half out the kitchen and *still* can't stand the heat
Not me—uh-uh!
I'm a rustler and a bustler
And a stone-cold hustler
I sweet-talked Fort Knox till they let me in
I conned a shark right outta his fin
I'm Sweet Sam DuPree and all the women love me
I drive a ragtop lavender hog
Money follows me around like a three-legged dog
Sniffing down a pork chop
And it ain't never going to stop
This here corner's my domain
I'm going to be here if it just don't rain
1-2-5 and Lenox A-ve-nue!
When the sun comes up, Sweet Sam is due!
I never break and I don't hardly bend

I got so much money I can buy a friend
I don't slip and I don't slide
If I ain't getting over, it must mean I died
I'm Sweet Sam DuPree
And *all* the women love me!

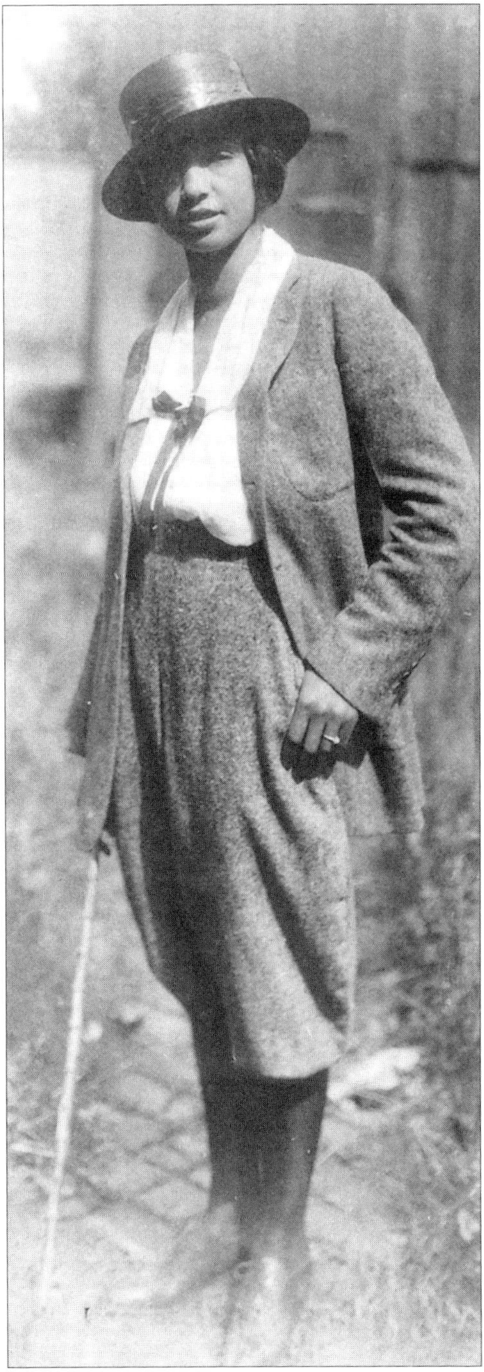

Clara Brown's Testimony

Part V

A young bright-skinned girl from Vassar College came into the restaurant last week asking for me. She said she had read in the Amsterdam News *about me giving away black history books and wanted to write a story about my life for a magazine.*

Well, the longer she stayed, the more fascinated she got. After a while, she was near busting open with the stories I told her. She said I should write my whole life story down and publish it in a book. She was proud of that idea, but I don't know. Me and her were sitting there having tea and watching the world go by. We was just two black women, but life had shined her all up and given her a real pert outside, while it had made me strong inside. She was talking to me like she couldn't see any of that. "Tell me some more," she said. I kept on talking and I saw she was listening hard, but I don't know if she was hearing.

Didi Taylor, 14
Student

I'd love to live on Sugar Hill
Be as rich as I could be
Then all the folks from down the way
Would have to envy me
I'd stick my hincty pinky out
Put my hincty nose in the air
Get a hincty chauffeur to drive my car
And a white girl to do my hair

I'd join that Negro opera group
If I lived on Striver's Row
And send my maid to the Colony
To buy caviar and greens to go
Mr. Van Der Zee would picture me
Next to my refrigerator
And if Reverend Powell gave me a ring
I'd say, "I'm busy, Adam. Call me later."

Or knowing me, I might go downtown
And live like the white folks do
Just write checks for everything
And don't worry when the rent is due
I guess 116th Street is not that bad
And I think I might stay awhile
Instead of changing the place I live
I might just up and change my style

Dana Greene, 18
Education Major, City College

Whisper my name to the west wind
As it blows across the Hudson
And I will fly to you
Screaming through the clotheslines
Flapping my banshee wings
Shamelessly over the bewildered streets

Close your eyes and think of me
And I will leap from the heavens
Onto your fire escape, my love song
Echoing from alley to alley
I bring my black and comely heart
To the tabernacle of your presence

Want me for the space of a quickened
Heartbeat and I will be a siren's wail
Tearing through the city streets
A lightning series of neon flashes
In astonished bodega windows
My love song cowering the city

Whisper my name to the west wind
As it blows across the Hudson
And I will bring you parts and pieces
Breathless moments woven into hours
I am the scorching Harlem night
Love's fiercest warrior

Bill Cash, 30
Boxer

When Letha sleeps
The sheet twisted between her thighs
And me sitting in the dark
Still thinking about the fight, the round
I should have won, the winner's share
There is no numbing pain, no reeling
Vision, no taste of blood, no feeling
Of loneliness hovering like death in humid air
Just the piteous specter of Prometheus, bound
And naked on the square canvas, the stark
Reality of an empty dream that only cries
When Letha sleeps

William Dandridge, 67
Mechanic

I have buried my best friends
All that is left are the snatches of melodies
A memory of me and Johnson in the aqua cool
Of the Baby Grand
Wondering what Einstein would have said to Bird
Over a cold brew
Me watching Bill Epps getting
Shaved in Ray's
Ray carefully navigating the ingrown hairs
As Bill reworked a nuclear treaty
Between Harlem and Russia
Like his life depended on it
Me and my buddies and a history to live
Through
Flickering images of our lives
Sports, the struggle in Selma, the killings
That nearly killed us all
Then one by one the long Cadillac
Ride to loss
And the sudden need to harden
To quietly burn and gently rave
I say that life is good
In the distant corner of my mind
A lilting solo slows
Revealing its bluesy roots
The wall clock revisits familiar numbers
But I have buried my best friends

Charles Biner, 57
Composer, X-Ray Technician

As a young man I dreamed symphonies
Elegant movements
Melodic flood tides on a moonlit beach
I dreamed of fugues and glissandos
Strings sobbing to the rhythms of Timbuktu
    "Oh, can you play a spiritual?
    Swing low, sweet hallelujah?
    Is that the right name?"
In my graying years I dreamed sonatas
Pieces that danced in my head
And lifted my heart
Great whirlpools of sound, and strong
Stronger than the burly new world
Brilliant brasses chasing seductive cellos
    "Oh, can you play a spiritual?
    Swing low, sweet hallelujah?
    Is that the right name?"
I won't tell them that they will
Never hear the mystery in my haunting
English horns or God's voice singing
From my tambourine heart
It is my black secret
And only my fingers, fumbling stiffly
In my sleep for some perfect pitch,
Betray me

John Brambles, 55
Numbers Runner

I don't sell dreams
I sell noise, a static buzz
That shuts out the whisper of despair
Sometimes for a day
Sometimes an hour
Sometimes just for the time it takes
To blink an eye
Between heartbeats

I don't sell dreams
Ain't nobody stupid
I sell a way for people
To lie to themselves
To weave the ragged fabric of a tale
Around a lucky number
A birthday, coffee grounds
In a cracked porcelain sink
Whatever pretends
To be a wall
Between today and insanity

Homer Grimes, 83
Blind Veteran

I shake my tin cup, rattling the coins
My legs ache from standing
A man claiming to be an old friend
(No, I don't remember his name
Or his company)
Asked me if I was bitter
What is past bitter? What is it that grows
Around my ankles and climbs
My rag-wrapped legs like vines lacing
Themselves against the walls
Of a dead man's house?
When he is gone
The air is cool, almost cold
It must be growing dark

Frank Griffin, 82
Veteran

If they hadn't been so far from home, he said
From Tennessee, from Mobile, and Duluth
Maybe I could have let them die alone, he said
Maybe I could have searched for another truth
Homer threw himself across that deadly space
They were Americans, regardless of their race
Never mind the bullets whistling past his flanks
He brought them back, heard their mumbled thanks
He was the greatest soldier I had ever hoped to see
He was the 369th, the Harlem Infantry
They thanked their God for giving them another day
But when their unit reassembled, they didn't even
    look his way
Sometimes a young bird flies oblivious to the fears
Sometimes a blind man cannot feel his tears

FEDERAL HELP SOUGHT FOR BLINDED VETERAN

Members of several veterans' organizations and civic groups voted yesterday to form a committee to seek compensation for Isaac Woodard Jr. of Winnsboro, S. C., a Negro veteran of four years' service. He had reported that he lost his sight following a beating by two policemen in Aiken, S. C., on Feb. 13.

Representatives of the organizations met at the headquarters of the National Association for the Advancement of Colored People, 20 West Fortieth Street, at the invitation of Walter White, executive secretary. Mr. White urged support for petitions to President Truman and the Veterans Administration to have the ex-soldier's case adjudicated as having occurred in "line of duty." When he was injured he had not served in full his day of discharge from service at Camp Gordon, it was said.

Lemuel Burr, 81
Veteran

Me, Homer, and Griff left Camp Polk
Full of ourselves, bursting with pride
We had Red-Balled across Europe
And had triumphed, not merely tried

We were already talking home
As we rolled out of Tennessee
It was late when we reached Batesville
We were the weary soldiers three

The Colored waiting room was closed
So we sat on a luggage cart
Homer saw the girl, heard her say,
"I'm glad the Negroes did their part"

Maybe it was the uniform
Or gratitude that made her speak
God knows she didn't mean no harm
When she kissed Homer on the cheek

But she was white, and he was black
And when that bus sat there I knew
There was trouble coming, Oh, Lord
Griff turned to me—what would they do?

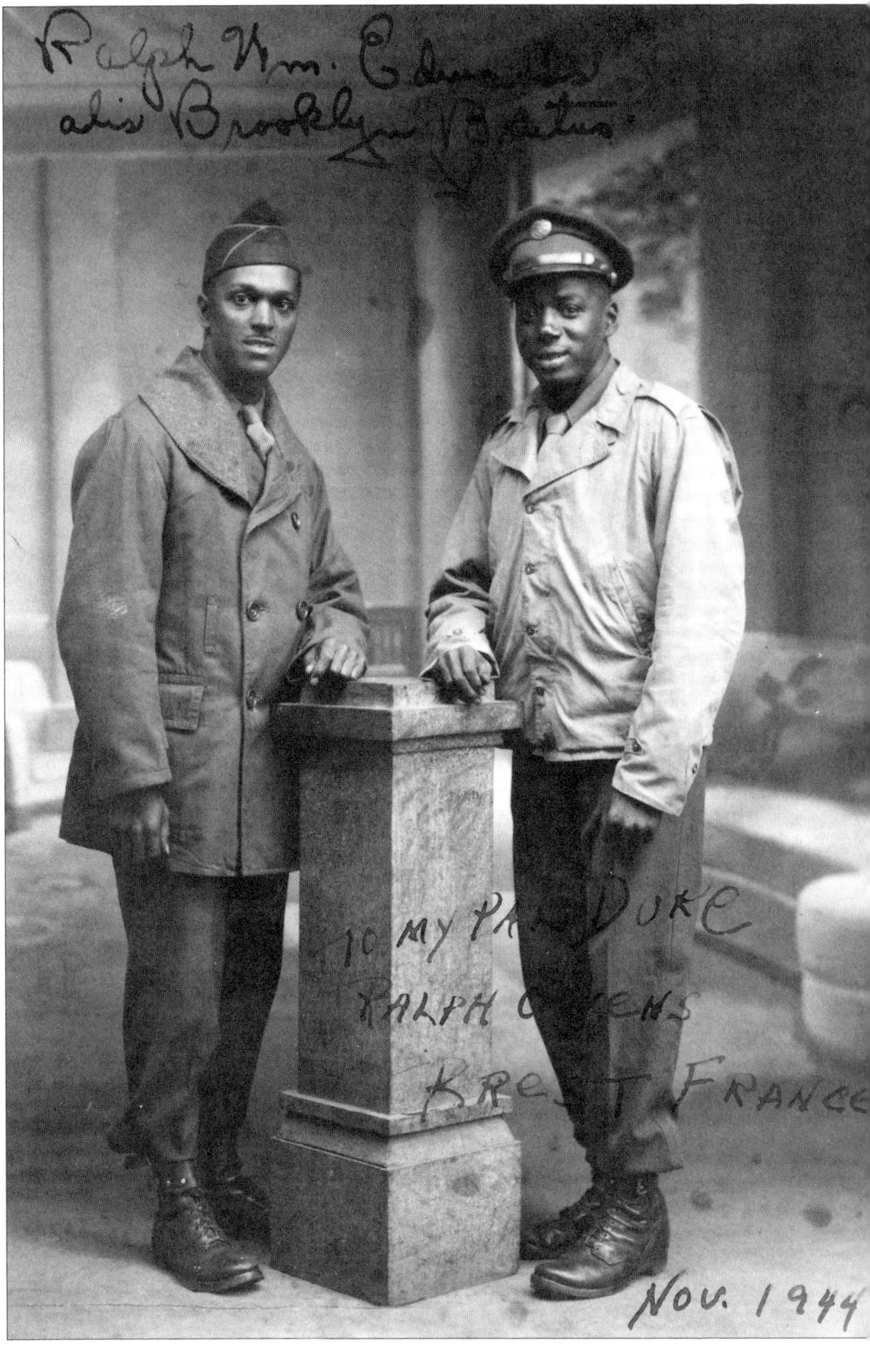
Ralph Wm. Edwards
alis Brooklyn
NOV. 1944

The girl cried but the sheriff said
It was going to be all right
That bus just wasn't for darkies
No brave darky soldiers that night

We had saved the world from Hitler
But on that dark road they snatched our prize
They pounded away Griff's courage
And they tore out poor Homer's eyes

"What can you see?" the Negro doctor
Asked as he tried to ease the pain
Homer said he'd been away awhile
Now he saw he was home again

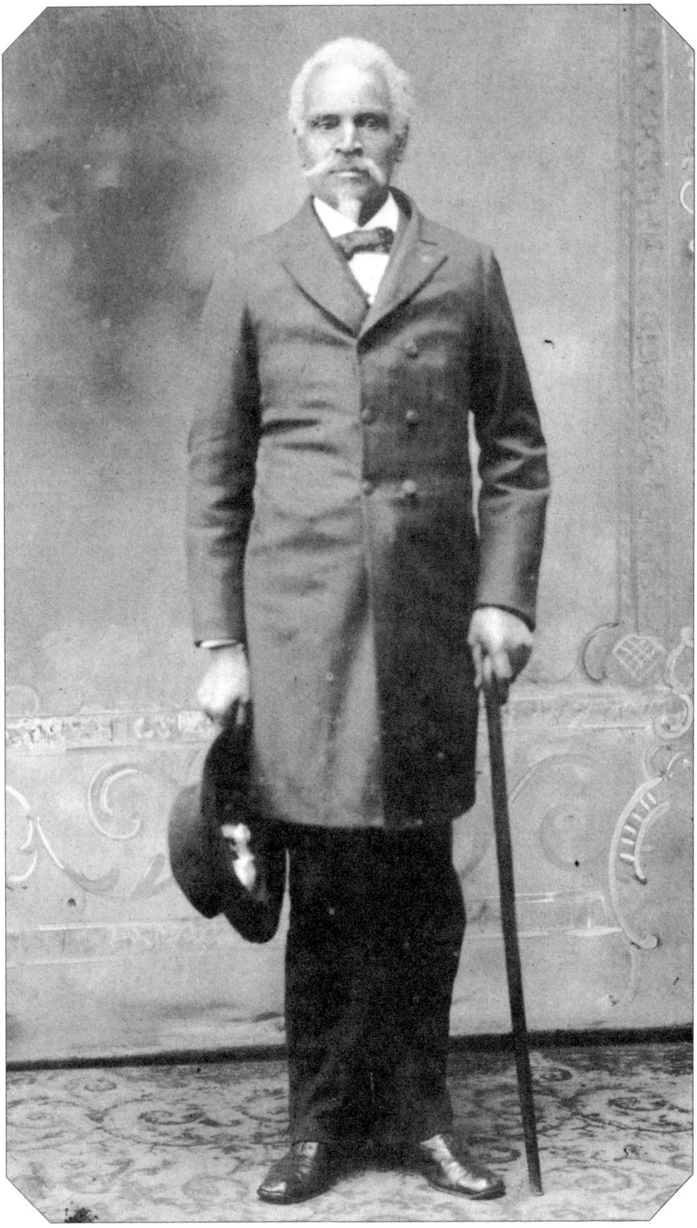

Clara Brown's Testimony

Part VI

Went to see Dr. Craft and he give me some pills. He said, "Clara, how long have I been seeing you?" And when we figured it out, we knew that we were what we used to call "old folks." Child, we got us a laugh on that. We were giggling so bad, his little nurse stuck her head in the door to see what was going on.

Then he told me he was worried about Harlem. He said we were too busy worrying about getting things when we needed to be getting ourselves together. We need to teach the children about being a community.

I told him not to worry. Harlem has been worse off, and it's been better. It's had its big-time people and its struggling folk. If it got to be one thing to everybody, either we wouldn't be black or it wouldn't be Harlem. Now, would it?

Lydia Cruz, 15
Student

I know I shouldn't do anything in haste
And how my youth is a terrible thing to waste
And I know that young boys only want one thing
No matter what sanctified song they sing
But, Mama, see how he's looking at me!

With his eyes crawling into places they shouldn't be
And him styling and showing off those pretty teeth
Like he's really not bone rotten underneath
That curly hair and sneaky grin
And is that a dimple in that boy's chin?
I know my mind is set on educational goals
Uplifting my people and joining the rolls
Of women with more than fun on their minds
And leaving dangerous boys like him behind
I know he's risky, with that big broad shoulder
Slanting toward me like he wants to get bolder
He can't change a thing 'bout what I want to be
But, oh, Mama, see how that boy is looking at me!

I might listen to what he has to say
Just so I can look back one day
And see all the traps your daughter missed
And all the foolish young men I could have kissed
If I was some kind of hussy child

Who every time she saw a boy just ran wild
And didn't know her great destiny
But, oh, Mama, see how he's looking at me!

Kevin Broderick, 20
Pre-Law, City College

When all else has failed me
When my crescendo of sound and fury has
Whined its way into the far
Crevices of this darkling plain
When I am less of me
Than the calculus of my parts
There is still the wonder of you

In your arms, I am.
In your brooding thoughts, I stir
To sprinkle the night sky
With endless galaxies of what might be
You leave the taste of love
Rampant on my tongue
A sweet forever feast

Earl Prentiss, 39
Motorman

My village, my village
The same scorch of sun that summers the Niger
Summers, too, my village
Simmering in its own heat
Ablaze with its own dark genius
As children with leap genes and Songhai anthems
Long forgotten clicks toying with their
Tongues
Dream that they are creating
The language their ancestors dreamed
An eternity before
They dance the dance of the Congo
To a scale that has
Survived the foam and fleck
Of the Middle Passage

My village, my village
I am safe here
Here where joy and despair
Sweat together in the heavy darkness
Where violence sharpens its eyes on me
Gapes me like a ravening lion
Here my soul is safe
Here where wailing bebop rhythm
Insinuate their spells
Along the wide avenues

And hard-eyed Masai women watch from
Third-floor windows
These are my people
My brown and holy earth
The same scorch of sun
That summers the Niger
Warms my Ashanti heart
Here in my village,
My Harlem

Clara Brown, 87
Retired

When I was young, I danced these streets
There wasn't no time for strollin'
I had to keep my feet moving, moving
'Cause it seemed like the music
Was just gonna pour out from the churches
And the music halls and SWOOP
Me up to the rooftops.
Oh, child, my legs are aching now
The pains come rollin', rollin'
And a pile of years
Keeps sighing and signifying
In my ear like an old friend
About my Harlem
About my Harlem
And it's all mine, you know
Yes, it's done changed some, honey
And rearranged itself some
But when I was young, I danced these streets

Some people, places, and terms . . .

Marcus Garvey (1887–1940) was a black political activist. **Langston Hughes (1902–1967)** and **Countee Cullen (1903–1946)** were poets active in the Harlem Renaissance. **W. E. B. Du Bois (1868–1963)** and **Booker T. Washington (1856–1915)** were important educators and thinkers. **Adam Clayton Powell, Jr. (1908–1972)** was pastor of **Abyssinian Baptist Church** and a popular congressman.

Sugar Hill was where the well-off folks lived. Homes along **Striver's Row** were not as grand. Some people had **rent parties** where food and drinks were sold to raise money for the rent. Often a stride pianist such as **James P. Johnson (1894–1955)** would entertain. The **Cotton Club** was a popular nightspot at 142nd Street and Lenox Avenue. **Sylvia's** restaurant is well known. **Jackie Robinson (1919–1972)** integrated modern baseball in 1946. **Charlie "Bird" Parker (1920–1955)**, jazz musician, played **bebop**.

Three important writers—**Richard Wright (1908–1960)**, **Zora Neale Hurston (1891–1960)**, and **James Baldwin (1924–1987)** wrote about black life.

James Van Der Zee (1886–1983) had his photography studio on Harlem's **Lenox Avenue**. The **369th Infantry** was known as the Harlem Hellfighters.

The **A train** in the New York City subway system stops at **125th Street**, the heart of Harlem. The **Apollo Theater** is famous for its amateur night contests. When black people were forced to sit high in the balcony, they called it **Nigger Heaven**. **Hincty** people are conceited. Walter Dean Myers lived on **Morningside Avenue** and is not hincty.

W. 146TH

2032

W. 146TH

MANHATTAN ELEVATED RAILWAY CO.
2031

W. 145TH

MANHATTAN ELEVATED RAILWAY CO.
2030

W. 144TH

2029

W. 143RD

2028

W. 142ND

2027

W. 141ST

2026

W. 140TH

2025

W. 139TH

2024

W. 138TH

2023

W. 137TH

1942

W. 136TH

John De Lancey to A. Wall. L. 2 B3 P.276

METROPOLITAN STREET RAILWAY C[O]
2015
POWER HOUSE & SHOPS

2014

2013

2012

2011

2010

2009

2008

2007

2006

1921

Peter Myer

EIGHTH AV.

SIXTH AV.

SEVENTH AV.